BUILT FOR SPEED

SPRINT CAR

Luke Thompson

HIGH
interest
books

Children's Press
A Division of Grolier Publishing
New York / London / Hong Kong / Sydney
Danbury, Connecticut

Book Design: Nelson Sa
Contributing Editor: Jeri Cipriano

Photo Credits: Cover, pp. 5, 6, 9 © Mike Campbell Photos; p. 11/Top © M&M Photos; p. 11/Bottom© IndexStock; p. 12 © AP/World Wide Photos; p. 13 © Mike Campbell Photos; p. 15 © AP/World Wide Photos; p. 16 © M&M Photos; p. 19 © Mike Campbell Photos; pp. 20, 23 © AP/World Wide Photos; pp. 24, 27 © M&M Photos; pp. 26, 27 © Mike Campbell Photos; p. 30 © M&M Photos; pp. 32, 33 © AP/World Wide Photos; p. 34 © Mike Campbell Photos; pp. 36, 38 © AP/World Wide Photos; pp. 40, 41 © Mike Campbell Photos

Visit Children's Press on the Internet at:
http://publishing.grolier.com

Library of Congress Cataloging-in-Publication Data

Thompson, Luke.
    Sprint car / by Luke Thompson.
      p. cm. — (Built for speed)
    Includes bibliographical references and index.
    ISBN 0-516-23163-4 (lib. bdg.) — ISBN 0-516-23266-5 (pbk.)
      1. Sprint cars—United States—Juvenile literature. 2. Automobile
racing—United States—Juvenile literature. [1. Sprint cars. 2.
Automobile racing.] I. Built for speed

  GV1029.9.S67 T46 2000
  796.72'0973—dc21
                                                              00-063899

CONTENTS

INTRODUCTION

You can taste the dirt from the track in your mouth. You grip the wheel hard as you round the corner. Your back tires start to spin out. The force from the turn knocks your helmet against the roll bar. Instead of panicking, you hit the gas and blow past the competition. The wind cools you off as you top 100 miles per hour (161 km/h) on the final stretch. The competitors are gaining. You think fast and hit the brakes for the last turn. This keeps you on the track. One last burst of speed and the checkered flag drops. The victory is yours.

If you wanted to pick the most unique type of automobile racing to watch, many people would tell you to pick sprint car racing. Sprint cars are small, but they pack a lot of power.

Sprint cars may be small, but they are very fast.

They race on short, oval, dirt tracks at more than 150 miles per hour (241 km/h). Fans sit close to the action as the cars zip around the track. Sprint cars slide sideways into turns and come out of them with roaring engines. This kind of excitement at the track is why sprint cars are so popular today.

What is a SPRINT CAR?

Sprint cars are small racecars with powerful engines. At first glance, they look like dune buggies or large go-carts. Sprint cars look this way because they are open-wheel racecars. These cars don't have fenders covering their wheels. Sprint cars are also odd looking because their bodies are long and narrow. A sprint car has a wing on top that is half as large as the car itself. Sprint cars have huge rear tires and small front tires. Odd looking or not, these little cars have all the speed and power that any driver could want.

A CAR BUILT FOR RACING

Sprint cars have always been designed strictly for racing. There is no luxury-model sprint car.

These sprint cars are taking part in the 2000 Knoxville Nationals.

They don't have cup holders, CD players, AM/FM stereo, or air-conditioning. So what makes up an average sprint car?

The Body

If any part of the sprint car has kept its shape over the years, it is the body. The outer shells of today's sprint cars are shaped the same as the shell of a sprint car of the 1920s.

There are two parts to a sprint car's body: the frame and the outer shell. The frame is the sprint car's skeleton. The frame connects all the parts of the car. It holds everything together and protects both the driver and the engine during a crash. The frame is made of metal tubing that is welded together to form the basic car shape.

The outer shell is long and narrow. The shells give sprint cars their shape. Sprint car shells are made of fiberglass, sheet metal, or aluminum. Fiberglass is stronger and lighter than sheet metal, but it is more expensive.

The frames and roll cages of sprint cars are made from metal tubing that is welded together.

Most sprint cars are from 9 to 10 feet (2.7 to 3 m) long. They cannot be wider than 4 feet (1.2 m). Sprint car officials measure each car before every race. Officials measure the cars so that regulations are maintained for each category. Cars that do not measure to the rules are disqualified.

A driver sits in the cockpit. A metal cage called a roll bar surrounds the cockpit. It protects the driver during a crash. Drivers sit near the back of the car. Their feet are just inches from the engine. The car itself is low to the ground. This gives you an idea of just how small these racecars really are!

The Engine

All sprint cars have eight-cylinder engines. Sprint car engines sit toward the front of the car. Sprint car engines are all about power. Unlike the sprint car body, the sprint car engine has changed dramatically over the years. Today's sprint car engines are so advanced that they can run up to 800 horsepower. This is more than five times as powerful as the engines in cars you see on the street.

There are two sizes of sprint car engines. A sprint car's engine size determines in which class it can race. Most sprint cars use a

Engine Size and Power

The total area of all the engine cylinders determines engine size. This is an engine's displacement. Engine displacement is measured in cubic inches or cubic centimeters. The larger the displacement, the faster the car.

Horsepower determines an engine's power. An engine with 800 horsepower has the pulling power of 800 horses.

360-cubic-inch (6-liter) engine. This engine produces up to 750 horsepower. "Outlaw" sprint cars, which race in their own separate division, use 410-cubic-inch engines. These engines produce horsepower of 800 or more.

One of the things that makes sprint cars so fast is their light weight. Most sprint cars weigh only 1,300 pounds (590 kg). That's lighter than most cars made today. With a 750- or an 800- horsepower engine, it's no wonder these cars sometimes fly off the track!

The Tires

Tires are especially important on racecars. A car can go only as fast as its tires will let it.

To keep them on the track, sprint cars have extra-wide tires with deep treads.

A car can stay on a track as long as its tires have grip that can hold it to the ground against the speed of the car.

Sprint cars use extra-wide, treaded tires to keep them on the track. The rear wheels of a sprint car are always wider and larger than the front wheels. Some rear wheels are 20 inches (51 cm) wide! All sprint cars have rear-wheel drive. The back tires are large and wide to help control the engine's power. Larger tires help transfer engine power to speed on the track. The smaller front tires help with steering.

The Wing

Today, most sprint cars have both front and rear wings. Only a few sprint car racing associations don't allow wings.

There is no mistaking a winged sprint car. The wing is half as big as the car itself. A winged sprint car looks as if it might lift off the ground if it were to go fast enough. Actually, the opposite is true.

A big wing sits on top of the car and a smaller wing sits on the front hood. The front of each wing is pointed downward. As the car races around the track, air flows over the wings. The force of the air moving over the wings pushes the car against the ground. This makes the car heavier. A heavier car sticks to the ground better. A sprint car that sticks to the ground can go faster around a track without spinning out or flipping. Drivers who figure out their correct wing position can give their racecars greater speed.

The wings on sprint cars keep them from slipping off the track.

Wingless sprint cars are still popular. Some people think that racing without a wing is more challenging. Without the help of the massive wing, a sprint car is harder to drive. The car can't go as fast without slipping on the track. These factors make wingless sprint car competitions a little bit different. Even though they are not as fast, wingless sprinters are just as exciting.

A Day at the RACES

A good way to learn about sprint cars is to go to the races. During racing season, sprint car races take place all across the United States each week. In fact, there are so many racing clubs and organizations that sprint car racing is a year-round sport!

A few thousand people pack the speedway stands to watch the races. Some of the championship races, such as the Knoxville Nationals or the Gold Cup of Racing, can draw even larger crowds.

It's easy for you and some friends to plan a day or an evening at the racetrack. Compared to pro football or baseball games, tickets for sprint car races are cheap. They're less than the price of a movie and popcorn!

Sprint car racing is so popular that it has become a year-round sport.

How Races Are Organized

Racing organizations sponsor sprint car races. There are thirty-five different sprint car racing organizations. Many of these sponsor races locally or within a state. Several organizations sponsor races that take place at different race-tracks around the country.

Sprint car racers race on a circuit. They may race every week at different tracks or at the same track. Each racer wins points for finishing a race. The more points a racer gets at the finish, the more points he or she earns toward the season championship. A season could be ten, or even twenty, races. The racer with the most points at the end of the season is crowned the series champion.

RACING AT THE TRACK

All sprint car races are held on oval tracks. Most sprint car tracks are made of packed dirt. Some tracks are made of asphalt.

Fans jam the Eldora Speedway 2000 racing event.

Sprint car tracks are not always the same length. Some tracks are three-eighths of a mile (.6 km). Others are one-third of a mile (.5 km). Some oval tracks are one-half of a mile long (.8 km). The length of the track affects a sprint car's speed and the driver's strategy.

Sprint cars race down the straightaway at almost 170 miles per hour (273.5 km/h)! The racers must slow down quickly at turns. They often send their cars into a sideways slide at 130 miles per hour (209 km/h). As the cars come out of the turn, their engines roar and send them speeding down the track to the next turn.

The action on the track is always fast and furious. Cars bunch together in the turns. They knock wheels and butt fenders. Sometimes the wheels get locked together and send the cars spinning into the walls. If you're sitting near a wall, you'll never forget your day at the races!

During a sprint car race, colored flags are used to send messages to the racers. Here are some of the more common flags and what they mean.

- Start/Restart Race

- Stop Race

- The Winner Has Crossed the Finish Line

- Warning: Wreck on the Racetrack

- Race Is Halfway Over

- Driver Disqualified

John Franzen of Brainerd, Minnesota, flips his Wissota sprint car in the first turn at North Central Motor Speedway.

Heats

Sometimes thirty sprint cars or more enter a racing event. There could be only one race staged, but then it would last less than one hour. Race organizers want to give fans their money's worth. To make the excitement last, shorter "heat" races are run. Heat races determine which racers get into the main event and race for the event championship.

For most sprint car circuits, heat races are ten laps around the oval track. The number of cars entered in a race determines how many heats are run and how many cars race in each heat. Twenty-eight or more cars will race in four heats and a semifinal. Each heat will have six or seven cars. Five racers from each heat will move on to the semifinals or finals.

The final race to determine the event champion is raced by twenty-four or twenty-five racers. Final races are usually thirty laps

Sprint car drivers compete in heats to determine who will race in the main event for the championship.

around the oval. The sprint cars line up side-by-side in rows of two. Sprint car races have a running start. They run around the track and wait for the green flag. When the cars are even as they come to the line, the green flag starts the race. Engines scream, dirt flies, and the fans cheer wildly for their favorite racers.

Today, vintage sprint cars like this one are used as pace cars at the start of races.

A History of SPRINT CARS

The sport of sprint car racing is more than one hundred years old. This is amazing because automobiles aren't much older than that. According to some historians, the first sprint car race took place in 1896. It was held in Cranston, Rhode Island. This is considered the first sprint car race because it was held on an oval track and all the cars were small, open-wheel racecars.

In the early part of the twentieth century, auto racing of all kinds began gaining in popularity. Besides sprint cars, there were speedsters, midgets, big cars, and the even larger championship cars. The only problem was that there weren't many places to race. No one was too eager to build a large, expensive

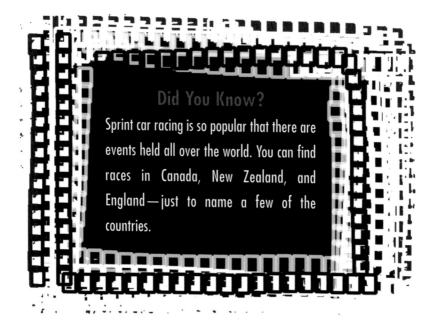

Did You Know?

Sprint car racing is so popular that there are events held all over the world. You can find races in Canada, New Zealand, and England—just to name a few of the countries.

racetrack when it was uncertain that auto racing could earn a lot of money. What if auto racing was only a fad? Instead of risking big dollars, promoters figured out a better idea. They began running motor-sport competitions on horse-racing tracks.

Eventually automobile racing became more popular than the horse races. New tracks began to pop up in several parts of the country. Sprint

Vintage sprint cars, like this one, did not have safety features such as cages and wings.

car racing was not even twenty years old before people began to organize racing associations. These associations would help make sprint car races bigger, better, and more available to the public. The American Automobile Association (AAA) was the first organization to support sprint car events.

In 1915, the International Motor Contest Association (IMCA) was formed. Unlike the AAA, the IMCA focused specifically on auto racing. More associations were formed several years later. There was the American Racing

Association (ARA), the Central States Racing Association (CSRA), and the United States Auto Club (USAC). Even NASCAR, the world-famous stock car organization, was involved for two years in sprint car racing.

Before every feature race, World of Outlaws racers do a "four abreast" parade lap for the fans.

These days, there are dozens of associations and clubs that are dedicated to the sport of sprint car racing. Among these are the American Sprint Car Series (ASCS), the Empire Super Sprints (ESS), and the All-Star Circuit of Champions.

The most successful sprint car organization, however, is the World of Outlaws.

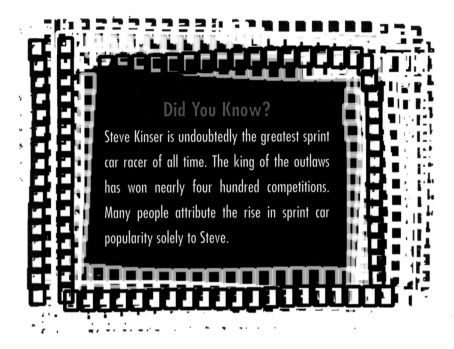

Did You Know?

Steve Kinser is undoubtedly the greatest sprint car racer of all time. The king of the outlaws has won nearly four hundred competitions. Many people attribute the rise in sprint car popularity solely to Steve.

World of Outlaws competes all across the United States. Outlaw exposure comes from television, as well. Although most sprint car racing associations cannot be seen on TV, many of the Outlaw races are shown on cable sports networks during the racing season. All of these things have made the World of Outlaws the most successful and exciting sprint car circuit to follow.

FAMOUS
Sprint Car Drivers

Let's take a moment to test your motor sports knowledge. Take a look at these names: Mario Andretti, A. J. Foyt, Jeff Gordon, Jack Hewitt, and Bobby Unser. At least one of these names should ring a bell.

Jeff Gordon has been the top NASCAR driver for the past five years. He's like the Tiger Woods of the racecar world. In 1995, Jeff was voted the Winston Cup Rookie of the Year. The following year, he won the Winston Cup title. Like many auto racers, Jeff Gordon got his start on sprint car tracks. Sprint car tires were his training wheels.

It's the same story with the other five drivers. They all started out racing open-wheel sprinters before moving on to different kinds

NASCAR racer Jeff Gordon got his start racing sprint cars.

Racecar driver Mario Andretti also got his start racing sprint cars.

of racing. A. J. Foyt drove lots of different kinds of racecars. A. J. was a great sprint car driver. He won many races during the early 1960s. After 1964, A. J. moved from sprint car racing to Indy car racing. He won the Indianapolis 500 four times during his career.

Mario Andretti is a popular name in motor sports. Mario's career started on the dirt tracks of the sprint car circuit at about the same time as A. J. Foyt's. He also moved on and up to race Indy cars after a few years. Later in his career, he moved to the international Formula One circuit. He was the world champion Formula One racer in 1977.

Bobby Unser is considered one of the best Indy car drivers of all time. He won the Indianapolis 500 three times. Bobby was just as impressive when he was a sprint car racer in the 1960s. He often went on long consecutive winning streaks. Nobody drove faster.

If you ask these guys what it was like to race sprint cars, they usually say it was the best time of their lives. There is something about sprint cars and sprint car racing that is more real than either NASCAR or Indy car racing. Some will say they loved the closeness of the fans to the track. Others will point out that the racing was more competitive. Sprint car racers love their sport and some never give it up.

At the Knoxville Nationals 2000, a fan gets to experience the thrill of the race, thanks to driver Dave Blaney and his two-seater sprint car.

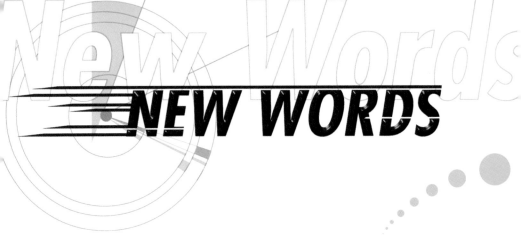

cockpit the part of a sprint car where the driver sits

heat the early race in a competition that drivers must run to see who advances to the final race

horsepower the measurement of a vehicle's power equal to the amount of power a single horse exerts in pulling, equal to 746 watts

motor sport any competition involving automobiles of any kind

NEW WORDS

open-wheel racecar any racecar on which the wheels are not covered by the car's frame or body

outlaw a sprint car driver who is not sponsored by a team

roll bar a strong cage made of steel that protects a driver during crashes

wing a part attached to a sprint car that forces air onto the car to hold the car on the racetrack at high speeds

For Further READING

Gerber, John. *Outlaw Sprint Car Racer.* Marshall, IN: Witness Productions, 1997.

Holder, Bill. *Sprint Car Racing: America's Sport.* Charlottesville, VA: Howell Press, 1998.

LeVrier, Philip. *Racing Kinsers: America's First Family of Sprint Car Racing.* Speedway, IN: Carl Hungness Publishing, 1989.

Sessler, Peter S., and Nilda Sessler. *Sprint Cars.* Vero Beach, FL: Rourke Press, 1999.

RESOURCES

Web Sites

American Sprint Car Series

www.ascsracing.com

Read about series racing news and learn about the top drivers. See the photo collections of the hottest racecar action from different racetracks.

Sprint Car Racing Association

www.scra.com

This site has lots of cool photos of sprint cars and drivers. You also can check out series points standings and see where the next race will be held.

Organizations
International Motor Contest Association
1800 West D. Street
P.O. Box 921
Vinton, IA 52349

Northern Auto Racing Club
553 South 7th Street
Modesto, CA 95351

Sprint Car Racing Association (SCRA)
P.O. Box 50937
Phoenix, AZ 85076

INDEX

INDEX

About the Author

Luke Thompson was born in Delaware. He holds a degree in English literature from James Madison University. He lives in Vail, Colorado.